someone forgot to mention,

Change is HARD

Facing Fear and Change from the

Mind of an Entrepreneur

Written by: Sharon Ehlmann

i

Disclaimer

This book does not reflect the opinions nor have the endorsement of any parties, mentioned or participating, in this book; including, but not limiting, those who assisted in the sales, publication, printing, marketing or distribution of this book. The information in this book is not intended to replace or substitute for legal advice. The author's intent was to be accurate in her findings, but is not guaranteed. We recommend that the reader seek additional resources, before coming to his or her own conclusion. This is an opinion piece.

Prologue

In her book, the author's voice talks to three audiences at once: the experienced leader, the 'wanna-be' leader, and even those who don't want to lead. If you are among the 'I don't want to lead crowd'; she urges you to please carefully discern who you follow, but know you can be a cheerleader. Yes, she is not letting you off the hook.

The author also urges the experienced leader and the business community to "pay it forward" in the **BUSINESS COMMUNITY CHALLENGE**. Give tribute to those, who have helped you along the way, by helping someone else today.

And finally the 'wanna-be' leaders, this book is for you. Sharon wrote this book because there are too many people out of work. Many are very experienced and talented, but there are just not enough jobs. It is time to create more leaders. As she sees it, if we want to save America, as it was founded, we need to plant the seeds to grow more American Dreamers.

Her goal is to teach the reader how to become a purposeful leader and follow their own dreams; all with childlike fearlessness. Make a change, be a leader!

<u>Dedication</u>

I mention most of the people I know and draw resources from inside the pages of this book. In addition to those whose stories I have shared, I want to express special thanks and gratitude to my friends and colleagues who were my editorial commentaries and (English and Espanola) audio readers.

You are all in my heart, Thank you.

TABLE OF CONTENTS

Biography
Sharon Ehlmann, Author / Business Consultant

Sharon Ehlmann just authored her first book titled, **'someone forgot to mention, Change is HARD'**; subtitled, '**Facing Fear and Change from the Mind of an Entrepreneur**'. In it, she poses as a 'Guardian Angel'; guiding the you through the changes happening today.

So who is this 'Guardian Angel'?

Sharon was the youngest child in an entrepreneurial family. Growing up, she and her sisters had newspaper routes and worked in their family owned photography studio and lab. Graduating with honors from Southern Illinois University in Architectural Technology, she won four design and technical awards from the American Institute of Architect/Southern Illinois Chapter in 1984. As an adult, she combined her architectural degree with business ethics and fine arts lessons from her father.

Ms. Ehlmann accumulated more than 25 years business experience encompassing business development, real estate development, planning, architecture, and construction. Her forte in the business world was working with her a deep bench of colleagues providing clear communications and proper coordination; important components to control risk and expenses for any project. But underneath his whole resume is her real strength unmeasured until now: The Mindset of Purposeful Leader.

Ms. Ehlmann prides herself in her unapologetic laymen approach in recognizing the positive in ALL people and encourages others to do the same. She's unafraid to take on the hottest issues in the country and swim against the tide of media influences. While media and others attack risk-takers, Sharon praises them. She not only deals directly with current issues with a positive how-to remedy approach but teaches big topics in a fundamental way, then motivates, inspires, and provides hands-on follow-up mentoring.

Sharon Ehlmann
503-317-7714
info@ehlmanndev.com
www.ehlmanndev.com
www.changeishardbooks.com

Message from the Author:
MAKE A CHANGE, BE A LEADER!

Having More Faith than Fear

Ask anyone who has gone through a major **change**, even if the net results are good, and you will find that there are always growing pains. My goal here is to guide you through that passage like a guardian angel. **The first step is to get past the fear.** Just knowing that you have a guardian angel can help you feel less angst. Those with more fear than faith will want to reject this, but it is essential to come to terms with this concept.

Many of us stay frozen in fear by putting up our own walls and stopping ourselves, more than any halting force from the outside. Why? Because we are too close to the problem - but we can sure see, point out and fix other people's problems. What's the trick? The trick is to depersonalize the problem.

Have you ever avoided something for hours, weeks, months, even years just because of some illogical paralyzing roadblock which leaves you frozen in your tracks? Maybe you procrastinate or behave as though you are unable to complete the task at hand, only to find it took just a few hours to complete once you tackled it. Do you wonder, "Why did it take me three months to clean out the garage?" "Why did it take me

1

two years to put up a shelf?" "Why do I always fight with my husband (or wife) about the same thing?" There are so many reasons why we just don't want to move forward.

What the question sometimes needs to be asked is, "What is the problem immediately **behind** the current issue or what will you need to look at **after** the current problem you are facing is gone?" That answer can be a tidal wave of new problems, many times moving us towards a glaring look at the root of the real problem: We really don't want to go there! We toss the immediate problem back in importance and avoid looking for solutions only to find the same problem resurfacing over and over again. Until we are ready to deal with the problems behind the current one in front of us, we can stay stuck for a lifetime.

All of this talk of facing fear can be quite depressing. To save ourselves from mind numbing theories on our weakness, I've chosen to focus on our strengths. This will offset our weaknesses. To focus on our strengths is a choice, and mainly an attitude. By not needing to fix our weaknesses, we can learn how to accept - **who we are**. Once we accept ourselves <u>as we are</u>, we have accomplished what many fight with their entire life. That's huge! I guess that is what they are talking about when they say, "You need to love yourself." Using your own strengths to offset your weaknesses can work so well that we become stronger people and our weaknesses have less power over us. As we move forward using our strengths, we become leaders.

What does this have to do with running a company? Everything! You've just learned the first steps of a good leader; focus on your strengths, then lead by example.

My Strengths

_____

_____

_____

_____

_____

_____

_____

_____

_____

Do It Now

You don't want to wait until everything is perfect to face your fears. Heroes and leaders are born when they act under the existing conditions. So whatever circumstances you find yourself in today; NOW is probably the best time to look your fears right in the face.

Where am I right now? Well, probably not in a whole lot different circumstance than many other small business owners. Many of us, like you, are struggling. Contracts are going on hold causing debt to income ratio to become unbalanced, investments are losing value. We have had to renegotiate with vendors, contractors and service providers. We have had to cut staff, reduced salaries and hours; which in turn is affecting employees with lost jobs, looming debt and difficulty finding new work.

How do we turn this around, together? Faith, perseverance and some great ideas; which makes it all doable. It's not the end of the world; catch your breath, learn from it and try again from a new vantage point. It's all about attitude.

You can choose to laugh, cry or kick the dog. Remember laughing is more fun and you are the new leader.

My Positive Attitude

_____

_____

_____

_____

_____

_____

_____

_____

_____

Lead by Example: Okay I'll go first, follow me

Since real estate development is momentarily *in the tank* for me, I need to accept the new reality and look for alternatives by tuning my awareness towards the outside, invisible forces that want only good for us. These invisible forces are outside of our conscious self and guide us in a new direction since we cannot see the full picture. This is a good thing. Those who follow this lead are positive, strong leaders: visionaries.

Some people reject this notion, unaware that the invisible forces of the universe are seen in what we call order, not appreciating the purpose within individual pain, suffering or strife. They cannot see the good within it. If you have ever wished for no pain or suffering in life, be careful what you wish for, because what you actually wished for is called leprosy[1], a disease so notable it was mentioned in the Bible. Jesus felt the most sympathy for those suffering from leprosy. With discoveries from modern scientists, we can see profoundness in His teachings never before realized from early times. Scientists have discovered that leprosy is not contagious as first thought,

---

[1] *'Where Is God When It Hurts', by Philip Yancey*

but rather it is the inability to feel pain. People with this disease, who do not have the ability to feel pain, hurt themselves to the point of disfigurement and even death. Doctors have found that pain is the only deterrent powerful enough to stop us from harming ourselves. Even with that, it can take a lot of pain sometimes to get our attention. So instead of cursing the bad, look for the open window of opportunity being created in your life. Avoiding pain many times redirects us to find good. Relying on old truths, I purposefully look to be led toward positive things, because it is the only place to find and keep true happiness.

As I look at the trends in my life, ideas tend to marry well into each other. Sometimes it's hard for me to distinguish which idea came first. As I hold off on real estate development, I pause and re-exam old ideas. Readdressing unfulfilled desires, I realize my old thoughts and occasional casual pursuits to help people start their own businesses have become necessities in this economy.

I've always enjoyed sharing with others my knowledge about the skills and mindset of entrepreneurship and believe it to be valuable information. Now more than ever, it has become essential for me to move forward and purposefully strive towards turning my knowledge into creating self-help products and consulting services. Whether this is a small detour in my life path or turns out to be a completely new direction, I'm not yet sure.

In the past, I never focused on being compensated for helping people start their own business; although if I had, I'd have the time to help so many additional people. It could also provide me with residual income. This would reduce the risk on my other projects in the future. From my experience, people that go into business for them selves rarely have this big dream where they would mortgage everything to make it happen. Most of the time, they are out of work and just have to figure something out to make a living.

Whether starting with no money, small investments or perhaps a large one, I will address people at their different levels. There are some for whom just defining a goal is huge. Others have their goals and a good part of their business plan together but are stuck and need help to get things moving forward. While others may need to go in a whole new direction, letting their original dreams go for the moment.

It's rewarding to watch the joy and outpouring of gratitude from people whom I have counseled. Now that I've redirected my focus towards helping people realize *their* dreams, I can take what I know to help many, instead of just a few.

What are my hidden positive opportunities?

_____

_____

_____

_____

_____

_____

_____

_____

_____

What is My Game Plan and how is it Different?

We've seen companies out there selling their business programs as a lifestyle; couples poolside touting the big house, fancy car, and yachts. It's so far from where most of us are today; it can come off looking like just another scheme. Using someone else's old cookie cutter business plan instead of following your own dreams has a low-success rate. I'm not offering a business program. I am giving you the mental tools to create and maintain your own business which is unique to you and help you work toward the life you desire.

While a lavish lifestyle may seem ideal, many times it misses the mark. Wanting the big house and yacht may sound good on the surface, but let's make a list of what is really important to you; it's probably realistically more balanced on an emotional and/or spiritual level too – not just material. Is your family your number one priority? Then you don't want to set up a business which would have you working 90 hours a week or on the road constantly, in order to be successful.

To pick and find your passion, pay attention to what you have set as your priorities and regularly reflect to see if you have your priorities set in the right order. Regardless of what you say, your priorities are what you put your time and money towards. As a proverbial saying goes, "You make time for what you care for."

My dad was a great example of this. He sent me and my siblings to parochial school when we were not at all wealthy people. We were very blue collar. If nothing else, one of the most important things I learned from him was that this was very, very important to him. His actions alone of where he spent his time and money taught me so much about what was important to him.

Your lifestyle goals need to have business goals to match. By having an understanding of the life you wish to lead or not lead, may help you from missing the mark on the big picture. You can begin to do this yourself by putting your thoughts in writing in the provided space within this book. As I walk you through a sequential approach to planning a business and lifestyle that truly meets your desires, you can create your own guide to self-create and self-direct your own life. Whether you join a team or create your own; I want you to learn from this book and set out on your own path, using the experiences of those in this book as a point of reference. Plus, have the reassurance of knowing that you have the cheering support of the business community behind you.

While this book gives a broad-brush stroke to help start and maintain your business, any master carpenter or anyone in the finish trades knows – it is the prep work that is the most important. Many times, it seems to be the missing component for the novice risk taker. If you compare it to parachuting out of an airplane, you will quickly realize that your preparation is essential. This book is all about the prep work for an entrepreneur: teaching the qualities and the mindset in becoming a purposeful leader.

My Priorities

_____

_____

_____

_____

_____

_____

_____

_____

Okay – It's Your Turn:
Program YOUR Story and YOUR Life

Before I go on with more of my ideas, I want you to come along for the ride. A very helpful tool in setting or re-evaluating your goals is to think and reflect on your story and your life. *What makes you unique and brings you to the point of where you are today?* Whether it is an experience with a job or an experience with a hardship; whatever **has made you grow**. I've had a blessed life, but many around me have experienced extreme loss and have had very difficult journeys. Just sharing those experiences in either, a written or audio format; acknowledging them and learning from them is such a commodity that many of us take for granted.

I have a friend who story is so unique, he was born in Mexico; his mother was very young and basically abandoned him. His grandmother took over caring for him, but really didn't want to raise him. He was abused by severe neglect when relatives, living in the USA, finally rescued him. For whatever reason, no one completed the proper paperwork. Now he's returning to Mexico.

This story is so important to hear especially today, with so much strife and questions being asked, about whether we should we allow Mexican people to come up here to work. It has become quite stressful, and although people have differing opinions, hearing an individual's story humanizes the experience and allows us to really look at the big picture outside ourselves. I have been on both sides of the fence, myself. Being in construction, I have been affected by it, in ways both good and bad. My opinions on this issue have varied throughout the years, and many thoughts come to mind about why things are the way they are. Sharing this story or others like them, may not only illustrate a personal story but a group struggle, and allows the group struggle to become personal. Stories can make a difference; prompting a larger examination, creating dialog and even open doors to providing solutions to pressing problems.

I also have a girlfriend who lost a child. She is successfully battling alcoholism, trying to cope and just to move on each day. Those are things I can't really relate to personally; all I can do is, listen and learn from her. Somehow in doing so, we help each other. I have another girlfriend who lost her husband, and another girlfriend who lost her mother after complications from her birth. These are all things that can take a lifetime to overcome, and sometimes we never do. But I do think that these stories need to be told and there are plenty of people who would benefit from having a shared experience. Maybe you can share and teach from your experience.

Everybody has something to offer. Take a hard look at what *you* have to offer. In looking back you can find and just *define* who you are, which can help set and *define* your goals; or look forward and define a new you. Is there something you want to achieve or is there something you really want to do? Set that as your goal. After your goal is set, we will move towards turning your goal (thought or dream) into reality. In doing so, we will need to figure out how that goal, aka idea, can sustain you and produce an income. Many times it is as simple as turning your hobby into a business. What you now do for free may be able to provide an income. That can be your gift to the world. Don't squander it. Some people have misplaced guilt in following their dreams, but I think sharing and shining our talent is what we are supposed to do with our gifts. If you doubt that, just listen to a bird singing out of your window and know it is his gift of joy. What joyous gift will you give the world?

My Life Experiences: How does it define me?

_____

_____

_____

_____

_____

_____

Looking forward: What is my new direction?

_____

_____

_____

_____

_____

_____

_____

_____

_____

Who is this Self-Proclaimed 'Guardian Angel'?

While studying architecture, I developed the processes required to harness dreams and pull them from the depth of my mind to the surface, then communicate those ideas on paper in order to share the concepts and make them real. It has become natural and enjoyable for me to help others do the same. Hence my company motto, "Turning dreams into reality". Whether real estate development, business development or personal development; the processes to create a dream and turn it into reality are universal. I enjoy weeding through the confusion within each situation in order to create a viable solution. I then turn that solution into a particular product or service. Juggling many ideas and projects is where I hit my stride. The past 25 years has trained me to be a creator, starter, planner, developer, marketer, manager, leader, organizer, networker, actuator and facilitator. My goal is to teach you those conceptual skills and let you take it as far as you can. If you get stuck, I can be available as a consultant, aka *'guardian angel'*, to get you back on track and moving forward. You can visit my website, www.ChangeIsHardBooks.com to schedule individual consultation or join a group session.

I'm going to share with you my journey and show you a glimpse of my world so you can see into my thought processes and discover what makes them unique. Thinking back, what I've discovered, when taking on a project bigger than I have previously experienced, is that I have less fear. Partially because in reality if I haven't been there in that capacity; I can't fully comprehend all of the potential risk. Therefore, I don't fully know what I'm getting into. I can only rely on my advisors or like experiences in the areas which are new to me. When practicing architecture, I also saw this behavior in clients, and humored when these developers came into the office with a difficult project. I remember thinking, *"If they knew the risk they were taking, they'd never take it."* Sometimes it's scarier to take risk within the capacity you're familiar because you understand the totality of the risk. If you just jump into something bigger, you can do it with no holds barred because sometimes you're just too dumb to know what you're getting into, and you just deal with the problems as they present themselves. I'm not sure if I should actually recommend it, but it seems to work often: a bit of purposeful beginner's luck.

Between 2002 and 2004, I co-founded a loosely held organization whose influence helped allocate $2 billion federal dollars towards developing a new Columbia River Bridge Crossing for the State of Oregon. All of this work was a collaborative volunteer team of influential people whose efforts would greatly benefit the economic growth of two states. This grassroots effort achieved far from typical grassroots results. We found and presented ideas to influential people, who knew influential people, who knew influential people, who could present our ideas to the superior authorities of the decision makers; thus having directives come to the decision makers from their superior authorities by the way of our influence. This is what folks call *'the good old boy network'*. I found a skill set where anyone can participate.

It is inspiring watching industry leaders giving back to their community. Yes, their volunteer efforts could lead to indirect self-benefit, but their efforts also would benefit the people and overall economic growth for two states. You too, can work towards own *pet* interests, network with like minds individuals, and showcase your abilities within your own community.

Most leaders I've seen do extraordinarily good things. Despite this, only a few people are aware of their efforts because of their humble steward-like attitude of civic duty. Giving back to their community and country to whom, has provided so many opportunities with which leaders act. If you doubt me, look at the dollar amount of individual giving in the U.S. This doesn't count many things leaders contribute and completing themselves through using their influence and resources. Many times their money and time doesn't necessarily go through a nonprofit but still provides for the greater good, as they reinvest their profit or risk their own capital.

My small company, in three weeks over a Christmas/New Years holiday, prepared a proposal which included over $150 million in raised capital including a board-approved term sheet. Plus, we provided a construction schedule and formed a conglomerate Class A team of companies which could handle a fast-track schedule. The personal invitation to this project was received into my office before I even had a company brochure or professional web site completed, so that too was developed during this same time frame. That project and those like them could create many jobs. Not only planning and building the structure but long-term jobs created over the next fifty years as companies occupied and staff the building, providing services to the community.

Responding to a short list telephone request for qualifications on a third project, which we estimated at approximately $25 million of construction cost, we delivered in three weeks: the major tenant, four minor tenants and interested parties for the capital, all without the land being offered as collateral. The owners on this project had been looking for funding for over five years, yet we were able to get bank interest in three weeks. All of these opportunities grew from networking. What's my point? If you have the right mental business tools, size doesn't matter!

I enjoy helping people. Whether it is helping those doing well within their industry who want something more, someone with a hobby who'd like to make a living at it, those without a clue to their potential or even my ex-husband. If my ex put his sales skills together in a contextual format, he could teach many others, which could move him from being a top sales person himself to creating an army of great sales people.

We don't form partnerships anymore. We just help each other in certain areas of various projects. When he needs help, which usually consists of bouncing ideas off of each other, I'm there to fill in that gap as an advisor or unofficial-board member. Just because he can sell, doesn't mean he has developed the skills in every aspect to package his talent into a program and bring it to market. If we need to collaborate on a portion of the work, we volunteer the non-legal opinion/information as pro-bono or we can figure out the amount of time we help each other on projects or simply trade time with each other. Be aware that bartering can be considered taxable income but can be offset with your trade/monetary expenses. Just like your regular monetary income and expenses, track your trade income and expenses. Further questions can be answered by IRS publications, an IRS agent, your accountant, or tax attorney. Whether you trade revenue or trade expenses these business relationships help build your network.

Many people think partners are the answer, but it's hard to find the right partner. My rule of thumb is: don't enter into a full business partnership with anybody until you have known them for at least six months. Good thing too, because I almost entered into a partnership with somebody and would have been in a lawsuit trying to get out of it. Just like choosing a mate, discern carefully what is important to you; do not just consider skill sets but ethics, personality, and style. It might be that all you need to move your project forward is to arrange performance based services, barter, contract services, or add an employee.

I also don't worry about sharing ideas too much either; because as you can see, having an idea and actually implementing it are two totally separate things. You really need have to have the passion. Most people with the ideas are the ones with the passion. It is possible that someone could take your idea, but it takes a lot of work to develop it. Although the work deserves its own credit, I don't condone developing somebody else's ideas. I think it is better and more rewarding to start with your own ideas or collaborate with the originator.

Anybody signing a non-disclosure/non-compete agreement should be honorable; if you enter into one, carefully consider the long-term ramifications. When I use these agreements, I feel they are basically are worth the handshake they come with, so I select individuals to work with who seem to come with an honorable handshake.

Years ago, my partner and I started selling used collectable apparel to the Japanese. Within five minutes of working with our first Japanese buyer, I realized that I must never embellish and that I needed to tell them upfront every possible thing wrong with the merchandise. It was expected. As he and other buyers realized that I was going to meet their expectations, the trust escalated, to the point that I could sell our used collectable apparel to them over the telephone and ship it without ever having to meet in person. After they had received the product, I remember receiving written testimonials such as, "It's better than we ever expected." The trust continued to grow.

From that business relationship, I became aware of the cultural differences between America and Japan. You can see it reflected in American media and commercial advertising often full of half truths and careful wording. Those of us living among this have become numb to it and accept it. Perhaps we have too easily forgotten that living life truthfully is noticed and appreciated. In doing so, it is uplifting.

Taking this attitude into a local planning department and disclosing the full risks and rewards of a development project, I could see the reaction in their faces as they quickly realized: she's a little different. She isn't trying to get away with something - she's not *bullshitting* us.

This is especially true if you're trying to raise money. At some point, after you get past the bootstrap financing (see Chapter "**Pulling Yourself up by Your Bootstraps**"), you may want to take raising capital up to the next level. If you are completely honest with people, you earn the right to be their fiduciary[2] if they so choose. Truthfulness is essential in order to become a good leader plus it provides for living a happier life.

---

[2] *An agent such as: a trustee, principal or a company director, who stands in a special relation of trust, confidence, or responsibility in certain obligations to others.*

How can I become a 'Guardian Angel' by applying my skills to help others?

_____

_____

_____

_____

_____

_____

_____

_____

_____

Changing the Tide

Giving gratitude, honesty, and trust makes work fun. This becomes especially rewarding when witnessing a *change in the tide* of someone else's behavior and receiving a wave of gratitude, honesty, and trust return to you as the recipient - even tenfold.

Once while working in an architectural firm, I helped a new city planner with code interpretation. He was so grateful he worked over the weekend and got our client a permit approved to, covert an old gas station island canopy into new interior space for tire storage. That means we got the permit in three days, including approval from environmental quality and the fire marshal. It was essentially an over-the-counter permit instead of having to go through the typical three months review timeline.

Another time while working for another firm, I overheard the senior architect talking to the Planning Department about a project where a national tenant was coming into a strip mall. The landlord of the dilapidated retail center was a local guy from a small town. To have a national company wanting to become their anchor-tenant (main tenant) was a great opportunity. The Planning Department said they needed the developer to submit a Master Plan with the highest planning revenue requirements in order to approve a new tenant. The architect tried to tell the Planning Department that the developer couldn't afford it but they weren't moving from their position. After the efforts of the senior architect failed to move the project forward; the owner of the firm called, followed by the project manager. They all had similar story lines, stating the developer didn't have the money. I asked the architect about the scenario and if he minded if I gave it a shot. He said, "No problem, go ahead."

I was thinking my odds of getting anywhere with the Planning Department, after three people already called them with the same story line, were slim to none. But I got on the phone with the Planner, who was making the decisions, and I purposefully spoke very calmly, softly, and slowly, "Here's is the deal. We've got a landowner who has attracted a national tenant interested in coming into your small town. This national tenant isn't going to go in and let this mall short change things. They have national franchise standards. That's their protocol. The problem we have isn't so much the money as much as it is about the timing. If we spend all this time required for a major review the tenant may not wait, as they could find a site that does not require such a long land use application timeline. If so, the developer will lose this tenant. Do you want that? Do you want them to risk losing their tenant because of all these roadblocks that you are putting in the way when it's for naught? They're going to do the work. You will see it when we go in for permits."

A clear and direct message got the planning review process waived. It's just amazing that when you give people all the facts they will trust you; projects will move forward and the *tide will change*. In return, you need to trust them and build relationships.

Even when your role is being the average citizen, you can lead the public and *change the tide* by thanking those who are taking risks and creating jobs instead of complaining. A common compliant I've heard over the years is displacing poor people from deteriorating neighborhoods? Even if people are displaced when deteriorating neighborhoods are redeveloped, there is a bigger picture. Without developers willing to take a high risk in such areas, neighborhoods historically become infested with crime and dilapidating buildings becomes dangerously unsafe. The high risk a developer takes with such a venture improves the neighborhood not only aesthetically, but in most cases provides safety for both those who stay and those who move. Those who stay and have the wherewithal to make it, benefit directly. Those who move into different neighbors, which are now affordable to them, typically move into homes that are newer than the one from where they came. Yes, they may still be in a negative market, but usually safer than the original neighborhood was if the developers had never showed up. Movement of property values helps poor people most, even the displaced, by providing safer housing and safer streets. Why do I mention this? It's to help you get a new mindset and vantage point; making your fellow business owners into your new colleagues and true friends.

As leaders, I encourage you to *change the tide* by **policing your own industry**, also. Those within an industry have the best knowledge and foresight for that industry. Plus, your industries behavior directly reflects on your reputation.

What is my industry battle? I strive in keeping the *fire, life, safety* (aka protection of human life issues) in front of the *green agenda* (aka protection of sustainable environmental issues). Don't get me wrong, the environment is important to me. Growing up, I was glued to Walt Disney TV shows and movies which taught me a lot of about the environment and wildlife, giving me awareness which in turn gave me a love and appreciation of nature. Walt Disney *changed the tide* for a generation of viewers. When I was in about fourth grade I proudly announced to the family, "I know what I want to be when I grow up. I want to be a naturalist!" My mom literally cried, "Please do something to make a living." I was caught somewhere between being a bit despondent to becoming oddly humored by the unusual and unexpected lack of mom's support. I wanted to make her happy, maybe she was just having a bad day. I reconsidered and ended up studying and practicing architecture then combined the practice of architecture with construction, planning and real estate development in the great Pacific Northwest. It is in my heart to take care of the earth. I think that's true for most everybody. There are places that people need to live and enjoy; and places that we need to protect and manage.

I vigilantly question to help guard (aka *change the tide*) against unintended consequences from parts of the exuberant green agenda, whose actions I have sometimes seen inadvertently result in increased damage to the environment or cause risk to human life. I want to be free to question, when saving electricity conflicts with safety. From my architectural background, I naturally place *fire/life/safety* concerns on the front burner. What if someone gets raped or murdered because of reduced illumination? I think that is a far greater immediate cost than the electric bill or theoretical environmental impact.

What are the unintended consequences when we add light rail by eliminating two lanes of traffic next to a hospital? In Portland, they have created one lane of traffic going each direction, light rail down the middle, with on-street parking, and curbs everywhere in front of a hospital. How is an ambulance going to get through in rush hour traffic when there is no place for traffic to pull over? I do wonder if people have died because they can't get to the hospital. I had experienced this first hand to a lesser degree when my son had a skateboarding accident. He hit his eyebrow and was cut and bleeding. It took us 20 minutes to go three blocks in an attempt to get to the hospital during rush hour traffic.

On a larger scale, I wonder about the true intent of the green movement. While in planning, I found it odd that elaborate comprehensive plans, even in small communities, were <u>mandated</u> by the federal government to the point of having to comply or risk losing their federal funding. One result of these blanket regulations required property owners with forested areas, to cut or become conservators of their trees because it soon would be illegal to harvest. Not that they wanted to cut, but since their property's market value was derived from their trees, were forced to cut or face economic loss on their property when their conservation became a punishment. As a result, many people who historically passed their property down from generation to generation without ever planning to harvest cut their trees; again, unintended consequences.

It's hard to witness a forester brought to tears while he testifies about the 'Biscuit Fire'[3] where loss of fellow firefighters lives, wildlife, ecosystems and thousands of acres burn out of control because of limited road accesses and undermanaged forests; to the point in which, this fire was fought in part on horseback. These loses, this forester felt, were a direct results of bad forest management policy directives from outside groups who trumped U.S. Forestry Departments authority, which tied their hands and prevented them from using historically successful forest management practices of negotiating cooperative partnerships with logging company for access roads and fire lines.

There are so many cases of good intentions gone wrong ending in unintended results, it is surreal. It's like green is out of control with a powerful narrow agenda almost having a total disregard for the consequences of its actions. It appears that since the USA is a member of the United Nations, we must adopt the international policies which have no inherent concern for our constitution. Those countries whose ideals conflict with our constitution can use environmental (green) laws to negate parts of our constitution which we take for granted. Many find it unthinkable to imagine that their personal property rights and

---

[3] *Oregonians In Action* www.oia.org
http://www.conservativetruth.org/article.php?id=118

freedoms of movement are being relinquished by regulatory agencies. It's almost like an undeclared economic war on the country using green supporters as pawns in battle.

What does this have to do with change? I use these examples to warn you how hard it can be to be a leader and *change the tide*. I also want to illustrate the battles many industry leaders face. Most of the battles are fought and won in the shadows of small groups, like the riddle of the tree falling in the woods: If no one is there to hear it, did it actually make a sound? I certainly hope so!

When there are inherent conflicts of interest (or when conflicts of interest start to develop), separating the tasks to provide checks and balances help negate these problems and avoids the increase government intervention. Hence, we are seeing *green* specialty experts separate and under the umbrella of the architect stamp. If dueling conflicting interests are not separated – carefully outlined the innate conflicts and decide which situation gets the priority.

Not seeing *the forest for the trees* defines many of our problems today; as specialty groups' step on each other, even to the point of derailing the original structure of an industries purpose. It is important to step back and make sure, maybe even define, the purpose (constitution) of the industry to assure that it is not defiled.

How can I police my industry?

_____

_____

_____

_____

_____

_____

_____

_____

Being a leader at the local level is difficult sometimes but it can be a nightmare at the national and world levels. It is endlessly challenging to be a strong leader in today's world where mass media denigrates whomever it chooses to target; if you become a leader, don't expect praise.

If you don't want to lead us out of this; you can help greatly by becoming a *cheerleader* to those who are taking the risks for us. As you can see, being a leader is difficult. It seems to have become *open season* for attacking leaders. My goal is to encourage you to *change the tide* from focusing on the negative to focusing on the positive. I don't ask anyone to do more than I am willing to do myself. So I am **leading by example** and becoming a *cheerleader* not only for <u>you</u> but also for some of the biggest targets in the country across: entertainment, big business, politic, and wealth. These mentioned, herein, are just a few major leaders who have done tremendous work, only to have their success minimized to become vilified and ostracized. I'd rather you find the good in others and learn from them.

A lot of information clearing the past condemnation of Michael Jackson (entertainment) following his death has occurred, so I won't elaborate. But it is a sad realization that it took his death for many people, to even consider, taking a fresh look at the whole life of Mr. Jackson, without presumption and prejudgment.

Sam Walton, founder of Wal-Mart (big business), changed retailing with a unique successful formula which benefitted not only his company, but its customers and stockholders. He was the poster boy of the American Dream realized, and a true servant-leader. Numerous business methods have started with Wal-Mart and spread throughout retailing as the new standard within: customer service, loss prevention, employee hiring, serving under valued market share, very competitive pricing, frugal spending, and sophisticated streamline management, just to name a few. Wal-Mart's major vendors are required to have their headquarters in Bentonville, Arkansas. Besides providing great logistics; imagine the tax revenue generated into his hometown – Now, that's giving back to his community! A great many pension funds invest in Wal-Mart. Bentonville is among the top cities producing the most millionaires per capita for the nation, thanks in large part to Sam Walton.

Company stocks, profit shares, retirement and bonus plans are offered to qualified employees. Many of Wal-Mart's jobs are part-time and ideal for retirees and the disabled, whose ability to get hired before Wal-Mart's business model was very difficult. Wal-Mart's team found value in older and other under-valued employees; then nurtures them into their full potential. As outside influences continue trying to create policies which result in stuffing Head of Household persons into the part-time employee market for the long term, they should instead take a lesson from Wal-Mart's model and faith in people, and match persons to their full potential. These naysayers probably treat their plants better. You wouldn't keep your house plant in too small of a pot. Don't do it to people!

Former Governor Palin (politics) faces similar polarization. Her successful record to close deals that balance the strictest environmental laws in the country with industrial development of large powerful oil companies has me proudly saying, "You go girl!" Energy and environment were two of the biggest domestic issues in our country. She's fought both of our toughest domestic issues simultaneously in the most environmentally sensitive state, and found: balance and success. With all of the opposition, it appears she has accomplished this without owing favors, giving her even more power as seen reflected in the good things she has done for the state and thus the nation. Alaska's isolation mimics, sovereignty. With its small populous standing strong against larger governments and corporations magnifies her strength not her weaknesses; providing valuable unique leadership strength for the national stage.

Being a leader who supports and rallies the positive of all people, instead of following the masses that attack the risk takers is so desperately needed today. Please stop attacking those who have achieved more than you. They are your new fellow leaders and mentors, please support them. Create a supportive network for yourself, as you will find that leadership can be a difficult path.

I challenge you to help *turn the tide* from the *witch hunts* of attacking fellow citizens to *cheering* the good in others. Movements are contagious. Positive movements create a challenge for us and others to do more for ourselves, our family, and our community.

I am very passionate about this issue. Why? It saddens me to think that I too almost fell victim to the pressure as the media, full of negative portrayals of business leaders, almost had me give up on my ethical ideals of valiant leadership years ago. As I questioned if my ethics and business goals could co-exist, Ross Perot (wealth) came on the scene, proving to me that very successful business leaders could maintain their integrity (Thanks, Mr. Perot).

Who are my Heroes? How will I cheer for them?

_____

_____

_____

_____

_____

_____

_____

_____

_____

The Business Community Challenge

Giving back to the community has always been important to me. My attitude is that you make "giving back" a habit *before* you make it big, or else it never becomes a real part of your life. Helping others learn the skill sets which have taken me decades of trial and error to discover not only benefits others, but is enjoyable for me, too. This is also my way of "paying it forward" by giving tribute to those who have helped me along the way. As you learn, I encourage you to teach others too. Not only does it help someone else but as you speak you will solidify your own knowledge, while at the same time helps build your own network of like-minded individuals.

Many business owners, including myself, have been preoccupied running our own companies - worrying about meeting payroll, keeping our customers happy, keeping our business afloat or expanding; while assuming others are doing their jobs, like educating our children in schools or being stewards to our citizens and community through government.

One of the first times I noticed something was awry with my presumptions was when I went to a parent/teacher conference. A teacher stated to me, "We don't have time to teach the times tables…" and another year hearing, "…kids don't need to learn long division anymore." Both of these comments came from a (public) top rated magnet elementary school. I was baffled.

When I heard the long division comment, I asked perplexed, "What do you do?"

The teacher proudly answered, "We use a calculator!" After a futile argument with the teacher, I decided to teach my son many things I hadn't planned; including times tables, long division, how to tell time, and the months of the calendar. This was in addition to the special things that I wanted him to learn that were important to me, like entrepreneurship, business, finance and my value system. It's disheartening to see our kids being taught to care for the earth, sex education, and almost everything from a fear based mentality instead of love.

I had also presumed government and schools were reflecting strong traditional American ideals and love of country. You know that *'American Dream'* thing. Now, suddenly, I'm seeing businesses and executives being treated as the enemy and evil. Many people in the business community, like me, I'm sure are wondering: "What's going on?" No one seems to appreciate the good that corporation and business owners do for their employees and communities or the financial risks they take.

As I see the attitudes of my community reflected on bumper stickers today, I notice a similar problem. Somewhere along the line, something changed. I don't know whether to scream or cry, "They're getting it wrong." I feel I'm echoing Rush Limbaugh, "It's the *American Dream*, not the *American Hope*. Dream is an action. Hope is not.[4]" It sounds cheesy to talk about it because I was taught this and its part of my everyday thinking. I agree with Rush when he says, "It's scary and sad that too many people don't know or have been told that it's out of their reach.[5]" Too many people are getting left behind and becoming disheartened and angry. Considering what they're being told, I can understand why.

The most important and probably the most difficult concept to teach in this process, is how to lose the "victim mentality." If you lead while feeling like a victim, it defines *vindictiveness*. That is dangerous and ugly.

---

[4] *Rush Limbaugh, "Address to the Nation"*
[5] *Rush Limbaugh, "Address to the Nation"*

Recently, I was talking with a man from Lebanon who is a first generation American citizen. In our conversation, he remarked that he thought a society resembling Ghengis Khan would be a good thing because of the order and structure within it. I was flabbergasted thinking, "Ghengis Khan's mantra was like, *'love me or I kill you!'* Try to imagine what that would be like. There can be no love in that type of relationship or society. How could anyone want that? That is not the leadership we need. Being able to live freely with a constitution protecting "life, liberty and the pursuit of happiness" is important. Please don't wait till we've lost it to figure that out.

Oddly, the next day as I'm wondering, "Why would someone who disagrees with capitalism as the foundation of our country want to become a citizen of the USA?" I hear on the radio, that only 57% of Americans think capitalism is a good thing. My question changed from "Why did he come here?" to "Why am I still here?" It seems the battle is getting harder every year. I even found myself considering; that maybe I should be looking for a place where the idea of taking risks to create jobs, a better life for me, my kid and the people around me is still a good thing.

What should we do first? As I see it, the people who understand the American Dream as the *opportunity* to pursue your dreams need to **teach and show** the concept those who don't; even if it is one person. However, we can't just *tell them* - we need to *show them* that it is for everyone. To do my part, just like when I had to teach my kid multiplication and long division, I'm teaching as many people as I can, the virtues of the American Dream so that they know, it is for <u>everyone</u>. Anyone can become a leader (that includes cheerleading) or business owner themselves. I challenge the business community to help create, with me, an army of guardian angels to guide them.

If you don't know where to start; use this book, or access my website address found at the end of the book, to be part of a group coaching session or schedule an individual consultation. We have already lost much of our manufacturing years ago. If we want to save the American Dream, it has become our job to teach it or I'm afraid being backed in a corner financially; our next major export[6] maybe our DREAMERS, losing America's greatest assets.

How can I give to my community?

_____

_____

_____

---

[6] *"Ballmer Says Tax Would Move Microsoft Jobs Offshore"*
http://www.bloomberg.com/apps/news?pid=20601087&sid=a3yutzL3x ApI

_____

_____

_____

_____

_____

_____

_____

_____

My response to 'The Business Community Challenge'

_____

_____

_____

_____

_____

_____

_____

_____

_____

_____

_____

I urge those participating to share with us your efforts by emailing info@ehlmanndev.com and we will post them at www.changeishardbooks.com .

48

Change is HARD

During the 2008 presidential election, I remember Obama advocating, "We want change, change, change..." and people responding, "Yeah, we want change, we want change..." Now that change is here, its like, "Wow! Ouch! Change is HARD!"

I was talking to a friend/mentor who lived through the 1930's depression and remembers it well. He stated several points: "The biggest problem in the 1930's was confusion...That's what made it last so long...We are in a similar mode of confusion today... the rules[7] are changing...We just need to let the rules go into place."

I'm questioning, "What are the rules going to be tomorrow?" My friend and I both agree: Confusion tends to have people standing still looking for leadership. So anyone moving forward can get followers easily. The best change for yourself is to start leading your own life and following your

---

[7] *Rules of laws passed by the legislation; which effect taxes and business operations.*

own dreams. If you won't, then please carefully discern who you follow.

Confusion goes hand-in-hand with control, as more and more decisions affecting our personal and business lives are made by others. Depending on your perspective, you are left waiting for either the *"axe to fall"* or the *"cavalry to come"* to your rescue. Waiting for the government to be your cavalry creates more dependency on the government, which by the way has its spending habits on steroids. Those who see it as an *"axe to fall"* know that our government with its insatiable spending habits is going to get its revenue stream fed.

Many people are scared by what's going on in the economy and unnerved by it. I don't like what's going on either, but I feel that I have my own game plan and that I am a bit ahead mentally.   Those who thrive during these times sometimes appear to be magicians. When they just have a skill set. To stay ahead when things get tough, your mind needs become like that of a soldier, persevering against impossible odds. Create and know your mission. Then rely, on that plan, to get you through the fire storm. Your plan should be flexible and creative. Prepare alternate plans, especially if your game plan involves high risk.

To defend myself from the world's fearful reaction to the changes, which are out of our easy reach to control; I just stop my exposure to the fear mongers by turning off the TV news commentary. By doing this, I can focus on my personal life and where I need to go. I also did this once before, about 24-hours after the planes flew into the World Trade Center in 2001. Overwhelmed with grief, I went into mourning. After about a year, I slowly tuned back into the media. I was shocked to find that America's optimistically fearless attitude had changed into "Chicken Little," acting as though the sky was falling and being even more fearful. As a result of continued fear mongering, I have accepted the fact that we are now becoming a country characterized with government ownership of private industries and an expansion of regulation and fees which are strangling companies. While companies still take the financial risk their new government competitor just prints more money. Plus coming soon to taxpayer's the unprecedented financial burden. This trend may change back, but right now that appears to be what the administration wants and what enough people voted for.

At first, I ignored these facts and drew the conclusion that I had to deal with the situation, rather than fight it. Basically, I would succumb to it. Okay that thought lasted for about a minute. Then I decided to create this book and present to people looking for guidance,

How *self-reliance*[8]...

[My definition of self-reliance, from my vantage point, is the act of trusting and relying on the sub-conscience/all-knowing/(Holy) Spirit[9] within ourselves and know it is part of the self (God with us).[10]]

...is the answer to self control.

Or as stated in the United States Code at 36 U.S.C. § 302, '"**In God we trust" is the national motto'**.

---

[8] *Emerson's essay, Self-Reliance*
[9] *Subconscious (scientific word choice)|all-knowing (spiritual word choice)|Holy Spirit (Christian Theology word choice)*
[10] *The Bible*

Game Plan

Look closely at what is in your control. Generally speaking, I think the state of the economy is currently, for most of us, out of our control. It's a new playing field. There are some of you who may be able to go out and turn this ship around, but for most of us <u>we will need to accept what is</u>; if not in **Plan A**, at least in a plan. My primary focus is **Plan A:** writing/publishing this book. Encouraging one person at a time to a continuing legacy which founded this country: "freedom to pursue happiness" or using the modern language of Nike, "Just Do It."

Plan A (coping strategy #1): *Lemons to Lemonade.* Instead of fighting the roadblocks in your life the trick is to maneuver around them and use the problem(s) as the key(s) to your solution.

It's usually what makes your plan unique. In architecture, I found this to be true. Restrictions on a site, like a tree needing to remain or a setback encroaching into the site, can at first seem frustrating to the inexperienced designer, but I found that the trick is to use the restrictions to define the project. The same is true with developing a product or service. Embrace the restrictions instead of fighting against them. Make it define the project. Discovering and using this attitude of embracing problems was the secret to winning my design awards in architectural school. It's what made it unique and better.

The same is true in defining my **Plan A**: Writing/publishing this book and offering consulting services.

Confront the problem: People out of work

Embrace the problem: By accepting the problem and make it the key component to the **solution**.

Analyzing the reason the problem exists: Shortage of leaders creating jobs/many over qualified experienced work force/job loss and finding the hidden benefit.

Solution: Give them something better than a job; turn them into leaders/job creators.

Hopefully the present difficulties turn us into a stronger country and world in the long run, but it will take hard work and good positive leaders to do it.

Plan B (coping strategy #2): *Reinforcements.* After a year-long search, I've signed an agreement with a granite and marble company which may help pull my floor covering installation company back from the brink. We will be working in cooperation to create a win-win for both companies. With many industries hurting, look within your network and neighboring industries that also have similar, but not conflicting services, or even the competition to see if new relationships can be developed. Pull your networks closer together to help each other.

Plan C (coping strategy #3): *Thinking outside of the box/Staying on the offense/Hard Ball.* This strategy is for advanced player and not the faint of heart nor the casual reader, so I'm looking for an effort. Plus it will help jump start your networking. To be part of Coping Strategy #3 you need to attend an interactive mock board meeting. The admission is free but would like it to stand apart from the business participation of the book as we *put all the cards on the table.* So let's enter the board room. To do that visit:

www.changeishardbooks.com/boardroom Password: **Plan C**

My Plan A (coping strategy #1): *Lemons to Lemonade.*

_____

_____

_____

_____

_____

_____

_____

_____

My Plan B (coping strategy #2): *Reinforcements.*

_____

_____

_____

_____

_____

_____

_____

My Plan C (coping strategy #3): *Thinking outside of the box/Staying on the offense/Hard Ball.*

_____

_____

_____

_____

_____

_____

_____

Growing Pains

Human nature likes things to remain constant. When the majority voted for 'change' during the 2009 Presidential Election, I don't think most people thought it through to realized, going through change, isn't always as easy as it first appears.

Growing pains occurs in many varieties – let's look at your life path, for example. Sometimes you may need to ask yourself, are you are on the wrong path? If so, are you continuing down the wrong path because you don't want to admit you were wrong? We all make mistakes. The biggest mistake is not fixing problems as we learn. It's better to, try and fail, than never trying at all, but lose the ego. It's unwise to continue on the wrong road because you're afraid of admitting a mistake. Research, reflect, learn from it and correct it. Don't be afraid of people knowing that you made a mistake. Growth is admirable to watch. My personal recommendation: starting your learning curve bootstrapping, not mortgaging the house. Even experience doesn't necessarily warrant burdening debt. Make your ideas prove themselves in net results.

Growing pains happens with implementing other ideas too. Like if you say, "I want to be an Olympic athlete," you enthusiastically start training and when it gets hard. You might say, "What was I thinking? I don't want to do this." You'll discover you're at the deciding point. Do you genuinely want to do it or do you not? You can say no, you don't want it, and you can quit. Or, you can say, "I really want it, and I'm going to bear through it." Sometimes we need help to make it happen. You may need to get an expert or research yourself before making costly mistakes. Moving forward is going to require huge growth. That's why even if you don't get to the end result; or the end result isn't the same as what you started out thinking it would be, the growth factor makes it so worth it. When you get there, you can look back on it and say, "Wow, what a ride!

What is in MY Control? How can I can I have more control of my life? How can I work around (react/work with) things out of my control?

_____

_____

_____

_____

_____

_____

_____

_____

Working with your Weakness

For me, creating business development services and product lines is the result of over 20 years of experiences, put together in a concise manner. My outlined plan for writing this book looked simple, even avoiding any new immediate capital outlay. You'd think moving forward should be easy, but did I hit a brick wall. Writing a book about facing fear and change was hard. Dissecting and contemplating growth and change are difficult subjects, as it moves me towards deeper personal growth simultaneously. It's like doing a virtual autopsy on yourself: curious of what's inside, yet afraid of what you'll find.

Going through change and growth caused me to have physical side effects too. Small stresses make me yawn which keeps my blood pressure low. You can pick up this good habit, too. When you feel stress - force a yawn or a deep exaggerated sigh to help you relax. Another healthy technique is laughter. Laugh often at yourself and your crazy circumstances. Water is another healthy coping tool: showers, swimming or even splashing water on your face as a quick fix. This project, at times, flooded my senses so greatly that I'd get sleepy, even to the point that it felt like I had taken sleeping pills. At the beginning of writing this book it wasn't unusual to write for two hours and need to sleep for four. Peeling away the layers of my thoughts, like an onion, was mentally exhausting; unsure of what old hurts or fears I would face in the self-discovery process. At the same time, I felt driven to conquer the challenge. I realized it was part of the processing for my mind. Fighting the sleep, at times, was futile. I had to balance the times where I'd fight the stress-induced need for sleep and persevere; verses just working regenerative sleep into my time schedule.

At some point when you realize you want to move forward, yet still feel crippled with fear, take a deep breath followed by purposefully ignoring your fears; bring them along as a SILENT partner. Then face your new life head on and you're moving again. Like my favorite childhood book, repeatedly read to me by my dad was The Little Engine that Could.[11] Towards the end the Little Engine chanted while climbing the steep hill, "I think I can, I think I can, I think I can," and as he reaches the top he exclaims: "I can! I can!"

---

[11] *"The Little Engine That Could" by Watty Piper published by Platt & Munk.* Ironically, Wikipedia.org claims that some would contend that this children's story, "…is a metaphor for the American dream."

What is My "<u>I CAN!</u>" Plan

_____

_____

_____

_____

_____

_____

_____

_____

_____

What are My Lifestyle Goals?

I have many business goals. But my current lifestyle goal is to be self-sufficient within a year. Remember, business and lifestyle goals are not stagnant; they change and evolve, as we change. What does it mean for me to be self-sufficient? I want to be able to live wherever I am in the world and still cover my bills and not depend on my credit cards. To do this, I want to cut my ongoing bills down as far as I can and pay off my existing debts. I thought the best way to make a living anywhere in the world would be on the Internet; so a couple of months ago, I adjusted my **business goals** to match my new revised **lifestyle goal**. Creating and marketing a product line, including downloadable books and consulting services, would provide the foundation I needed to move towards the life I wished to lead.

My Lifestyle Goals

_____

_____

_____

_____

_____

_____

_____

My Business Goals

_____

_____

_____

_____

_____

_____

_____

_____

_____

_____

_____

_____

_____

Leap of Faith

After lifestyle and business goals are established, we need to set a timeline. I am driven by deadlines. Look at any successful venture and you'll find benchmarks. Benchmarks are mini goals with deadlines. Progress checkpoints help to keeps things moving forward and the team together. If you personally don't have any mandated timeline, I'm setting a group target goal date of April 1st; it's an arbitrary date which has a secret agenda. My personal goal is actually November 1st; which is only fair since I've got a head start, plus it's the start of the Christmas season. Why didn't I want to use January 1st as my date? It's sort of like a New Year's resolution, which fizzles out because it marks a beginning, not an end. If you select that date for yourself; view it as a Year End to finish.

Benchmark dates should be purposeful. I wanted to pick a specific date to get your attention. The date can have many meanings. April 1st can be used as a tool against the unsupportive people in your life; the ones with fear and doubt who retaliate with condemnations. We all have them. The worst ones may even be the closest to you. If your life is full of supportive people, you are blessed. This is why networking is so important; join forces with people on the same page to help set the tone of your environment. Let the unsupportive people in your life think it's a joke, even call you a joke. It's okay. It's your dream and no one can take that from you unless you let them. You can be the last one laughing. Whatever happens or however it turns out, I guarantee you will learn something, probably a lot, including a lot about yourself. Remember negative people are reacting from their own fear. You are the new leader, fearless and full of faith.

What I need to do to get to that end goal by November 1st is to be very flexible. My flexibility started a few years ago when I wanted to provide myself an emergency back-up plan. This was especially important since I'm divorced and have a child. The instability of my career choice caused my mortgage obligation to become too risky, so I rented out my house. There were other reasons, too. The gap of the monthly mortgage payment verses the rent payment was widening to the point that I questioned the validity of ownership. My house was more like a starter home. Launching into real estate development, I had to ask myself, "Why should somebody give me their money to invest when a starter home was all I have to show for my life successes?" Even though I had a lot of equity and years of experience helping others become wealthy (or wealthier), I hadn't yet received large compensation for my own efforts.

When something doesn't make fiscal sense I don't blame an investor for questioning it. So moving into an affluent neighborhood with the flexibility of renting verses a mortgage, a clear business image and growth plan, plus a great environment for my son who was going into high school soon, wasn't a hard decision for me. Our old neighborhood street was safe enough while he was young, but I worried about the problems in the neighborhood as he got older and his world became larger than our street. He's quite a leader and I didn't want environmental influences molding him into leading the wrong thing. I feel that our environment, whether exposure to crime or the attitudes of individuals, influences behavior. No matter what the neighborhood or socioeconomic background; it is important to keep positive influences around you. Limit, even eliminate, the exposure of the negative influences in your life.

My mom taught me in rearing children that your effluence is enormous until about age twelve. After that, it is watching what your effluence produced. When my son was younger I talked to him about the schools that would be good for him. Then when he was twelve I could say, "What high school would you like to go to?" and of course I knew that the odds were good that my influence would prevail and he would probably pick one of the four that I had mentioned. It worked. I'm not sure whether we made the move because I had so much faith in the plan, or that I was backed into a corner and just needed to fight my way out. Because when we moved, I had no paying job or clients; but I still always worked towards developing my own projects even without financial strength. I had been out of salaried work for over a year with a thick portfolio. I was like, "What's up with this picture?" I think it's the address, the zip code. People will deny it, but I still think it had a lot to do with it. I moved and landed a contract immediately.

Even though moving wasn't a hard decision for me, my (invisible to my kid) boyfriend at the time panicked and wanted to break up with me because he was "too worried for me." He was one of those people that didn't have faith. Maybe it did seem crazy and extreme, but I had enough information to make my choice. One thing that will stop fear is having enough information. If you just walk in and see someone cutting into somebody, you'd be like, "What are you doing?!" When you find out he's a surgeon, your reaction changes. When someone doesn't support your dreams, it may be because they don't have the same information you have. They really may not know that you can do it and are reacting from their own fear. Keep that in mind when you go to people and ask for advice and counsel. Use advisors whom you value, that value you and who know your strengths and weaknesses. You need to be the final decision maker, because sometimes even your family isn't there for support. I've done so many things without support of others, as people tried to put me in a box, classifying the limits of my worth. I've even been doubted by my great loving parents, whose love for me was reflected by their becoming too worried about me. But they need not worry because unbeknownst to them, they set the foundation for me. It comes from within and having *The Little Engine that Could*, "I CAN!" attitude that I still walk with today.

Benchmarks: for My "I CAN!" Plan

_____

_____

_____

_____

_____

_____

_____

_____

_____

_____

Designing Backward

To help muddle through the maze of your thoughts, I've found focusing on the end goal first and working your way backwards helps avoid losing sight of the goal and clearly defines your plan. Attack each step slowly. Then go back and forth, checking your progress.

Of course, you can do it faster if you have a team. This quickly raises the outcry, "But I don't have any money!" If you're without money you'll have to build into your plan how the money required will be raised or earned.

Another key component for a successful business is developing business relationships, not only in marketing and sales but producing and financing projects. Bartering is a creative way to pay for necessary services and products. It also preserves your resources. Set proper upfront fees in order to perform work through accepting: credit cards, retainers, deposits for material, allocating for mobilization costs, or consider joint ventures. These are all tools to help make things happen and keep you from carrying the debt on you and your creditability. Pre-sales can work too; obtain deposits or *factor* (only if you must) your purchase orders. Providing credit can be risky and expensive to you. Qualify the customer and build-in the carrying cost.

When you make, set, and develop your plan; the fund-raising tools, as those mentioned above, should be put into the plan which will allow you to perform on a contract and get you to the money you need. People in business are doing this all the time, while carrying tremendous debt. If you're working with no money, at least you're at zero; you're in a better position than many others. Don't fret, if you don't know; ask questions and find out. When I am researching a new subject, many times I look for answers from three trusted resources before making a decision. Ask yourself the hard questions and develop a plan to resolve them. Looking at and preparing for potential problems, may help avoid them. Then if they do occur, your preplanning will help you get through the rough patches. Relax because when your plan is orchestrated, your plan will dovetail seemingly automatically. I design the path of the process first than follow with the financial components. If you find this difficult, pretend you are writing it for someone else. This will allow more detachment and you'll be able to look objectivity even creatively at finding solutions.

What is my Goal? Design the path to it backwards.

_____
_____
_____
_____
_____
_____
_____
_____
_____
_____
_____
_____
_____
_____
_____
_____
_____
_____
_____
_____
_____
_____
_____
_____

The Critic

When I started recording this project, my son was not very supportive saying, "This is your worst idea ever," and I'd kick him out. It would be nice to have the support of those around you, but sometimes you won't. I've had this idea for awhile, but I didn't even give it any serious thought until recently. All I needed to do was hook up the equipment and make it happen. For me, taking on a lot of new things at one time had me lacking immediate courage to examine the question, "What do I need to do to make this happen?" much less, the "what if?" questions that follow. Even though there were no life-threatening risks, I was behaving as though there were, frozen in my tracks. Regardless if the thoughts filling my head were reasonable concerns, I knew frozen in my tracks was not a good answer.

So one morning, I just started plugging in the equipment to see what worked. I still didn't know how to edit an audio recording. I didn't know how to tape audio on the computer. But it seems I had all the basic skill sets from general computer knowledge to get started. Now, it was just a matter of implementing the idea.

I began plowing through and trying to make it happen. I knew eventually I had to implement many different tasks. But to move forward, I had to initially concentrate on one thing at a time and ignore thoughts of trying to sell my house, negotiate a cooperative venture and paying my bills. I figured I'd write the business plan as I progressed. I hadn't even written down the thoughts in my head but just figured I needed to just get things moving, and when I saw some progress I'd start organizing. I had all these great ideas, and then when I sat in front of the computer I couldn't think of a thing to say. It was like listening to crickets. But after two hours of talking into a microphone to an empty room full of my "invisible friends", I started to get a lot more comfortable, even enjoying this new experience. I figured out how to scoot through and audio record on a webcam (two buttons start and stop).

After I gathered enough taped material, I began to transfer the audio clips into Microsoft Movie Maker for the first time. Little successes compounded, and I actually surprised myself. Eventually, I even got my kid's interest as he peeked through the door, noticeably eavesdropping. Its fun to watch the unsupportive slowly come around and become your biggest fans. As they see you take risks, they learn confidence and become able to believe in their own ideas too. By your own action, you'll not only lead but teach others to lead.

When the recording was complete I needed to have my audio clips typed. Then I had to organize and edit the typed clips, and put my thoughts together to formulate a book. I lightly outlined my "to-do" list starting with the end goal first. Creating, the steps to get me there; but I purposefully did not dwell on the list too long and dove into new tasks in order to start turning my thoughts into reality than grew on the structure of the plan as I progressed. Since writing a book and marketing it, is two separate efforts; I approached them very separately. I never heard of an ISBN code before starting but with Internet research and asking questions, I learned all the steps I needed to self-publish. I obtained a copyright, ISBN code, barcode, and built a website with a shopping cart. I learned the basics of search engine optimization, blogging, social networking. All were processes which were foreign to me. I never even heard most of the terms before I had started this project. I would learn enough to scoot my product to market than from initial sales, I'd outsource these tasks to professionals who specialize in these services as needed, to amplify the results. In doing so, I'd understand the basics on this new technology to communicate clearly and more effectively.

I researched book printing, distribution, shipping, bill processing, public relations and marketing. Then I had to implement the plan from my research and sell some books! To avoid costly mistakes, I researched book publication before trying to align with a book publisher. I realized also that I may not attract an established publisher and may need to build my own publishing team. In the process of building a publishing team, I expanded beyond the norm and asked the business community to participate. This not only was a creative way to raise the capital needed to promote the book; it more importantly, illustrated to the reader, the cheering support and encouragement that I knew the community truly wished for you.

Problem | Solution

_____

_____

_____

_____

_____

_____

_____

_____

_____

The "To Do" List

We are always changing. We need to adjust our business plan to our new and ever-changing conditions, keeping it a live document. Business Plans are not something that you put together, taking months and months to complete, and then put it away and say, "Now I'm going to go out and do my business." It's really almost like a "To Do" list. You should look at it that way and modify it every day. Call it your "to do" list and keep the end goal in mind. Start off with where you want to be at the end. It doesn't have to be just one document, because you might have several goals. It might be to get your kids through college, enjoy life more, have a lot of money, or maybe you want to change the world.

To do this might require you to take several different avenues and segregate them accordingly. When you get so many irons in the fire you may need someone to help you. How are you going to delegate things? How are you going to organize your thoughts: per dated benchmarks or by task or team member?

When you are first starting off, focus on your strengths and diminish your weaknesses by adding a team member (employee, service provider, consultant, partner, advisor, or board member) where you're weakest. Plan how you can build your team; whether you are hiring staff, collaborating with other companies or independent contractors, contracting temporary services, trade, goodwill, commissions, joint venture, company equity or ownership share. Having a "To Do List" style business plan will allow you to track progress, adjust to the changes and keep your eye on the final goal.

Team Member | Task | Timeline

_____

_____

_____

_____

_____

_____

_____

_____

Herding Cats

When growing up, my dad gave me very few rules. So when he gave me a rule, I knew it was important. That's how I live my life and manage people. I work with a lot of smart, well educated people. A former architectural boss of mine called this management style, "herding cats." This is especially true for experienced members of your team. You will have to set up check points (benchmarks) and clearly communicate to verify that everyone is on the same team, working for a common goal. By not having the "*keep them under your thumb*" philosophy, your team members are all going to do the job their own way. You have to take all of their work and coordinate it together to finish the project. It can seem a little out of control from the outside, but I do think it allows people within your organization to feel freer and less confined. My goal is to have people enjoy their work and really be inspired to do their best; which may make the product or service better than you originally imagined. As an employer, you want to be a guiding force. In my estimation, the company's atmosphere comes from the top down; no matter how large or small your company is, the standards and ethics you set and display will carry throughout your whole company. I put high expectations on everybody reading this book when looking to becoming our new leaders. Be aware of your influence and power; and use it for good. Heartfelt tokens of appreciation to your team and customers can go a long way. Be fair, even generous in your compensation but be aware that giving public recognition of ideas from others and verbal support of a job well done can mean even more than monetary rewards.

Whatever your most important philosophy or standard (safety, customer service, etc.) is, monitor that along the team like a chain. Be aware of the weakest links in the chain and build into your plan reinforcements in these locations.

Team | Motivation | Trade | Deal | Compensation

_____

_____

_____

_____

_____

_____

_____

_____

_____

Irons in the Fire

It's common for small companies to get so bogged down in performing on a contract that we stop marketing, which can send workloads into extreme highs and lows. Or maybe it turns into another year were you find that you can't seem to make your dream to be more than a wishful thought. Allowing enough time for planning can help avoid these problems. My schedule runs 24 hours, 7 days a week. It used to be 8 hours but I had so many things on my "to do" list, that the only way I could get everything done was if I didn't sleep. Now I schedule 8 hours of sleep. Keep a time sheet and evaluate it to see how you can make your time more efficient. My dad was highly disciplined in managing his time. Even now, I could probably tell you what he's doing at any time of the day. He had so much order and structure in his life, that it drove me crazy when I was young. Today, I realize its intrinsic value and duplicate it in my life, striving to balance creativity and flexibility with essential order and structure. Creating an efficient itemized schedule gives order, routine, and structure which can help fight against lazy or un-organizational habits. Without disciplined organization and time management, your company could fail. To help organize your thoughts, put your thoughts in writing or recorded them. Talking out loud is helpful, especially for females. We need to hear ourselves in order to reflect. Talking around ourselves in a circle allows us to come up with our own solutions. Recorded conversation conserves time, provides accuracy, and helps us reflect, organize, and motivates us to move forward.

Networking is so important, as it will become invaluable for every aspect of your company, especially offsetting the weaker parts. I ran into someone who was becoming an author. We were producing complementary subject matter, and offered to help sell each other's books. I could have started off just selling their product, but the entrepreneur in me thought, "I'm not going to do all this work without marketing my product too. We could co-market each other's projects and be strong as a team. I can fulfill my dreams while fulfilling his/hers and make money from both." If I had no other income, I might have taken his/hers product and marketed it, and at my leisure produced my product to add to it. But since I already had other sources of income, I didn't want to get distracted with something that might prevent me from completing my own project. Remember, prioritize your life and take the steps to get to your end goal.

I approach new projects by simply making a list of the things that need to be done, and then decide which ones I could do myself and which require outsourcing. As a designer, I have this desire to write ideas on a napkin or scratch paper, but the project manager in me knows that I've got to take that information and put it in my computer, make a hard copy, and get it filed properly. Your file system can start relatively simply. When I had the floor covering business I used a desktop calendar for a schedule instead of the computer, so when I'd get a call late at night I didn't have to get on my computer. All I had to do was grab my calendar.

Plan and allow for your system to grow and develop in complexity, as your project or company grows. Have a container, area, or work space for each task. Discover what your operational flow will look like and create the space to match. Find the balance between simple and complex to optimize the function of the system. Use what works; if you're having problems with your system don't blame yourself for being too lazy, just look at creating an organizational system that works for you, not against you.[12] Much of this will take trial and error, but give it purposeful thought. You will benefit tremendously from the effort.

---

[12] *"Organizing from the Inside Out" By Julie Morgensern*

Need irons in the fire? Contact businesses that you find interesting and find out their biggest problems. You might be able to fix them. Interview them and learn a lot about business. Find out what works and does not work for them. The same is true for existing companies. Go to your existing customer base or target a customer base you'd like to work with, talk to them about the problems they are having. You may be able to help each other by finding a solution to their problem while increasing your own business volume, plus strengthen your business relationship with them at the same time.

Client | Problems | Solutions

_____

_____

_____

_____

_____

_____

_____

_____

_____

_____

_____

Pulling Yourself Up By Your Bootstraps

Before you think re-training is your only option, take stock of the knowledge and skills you already bring to the table. Some years ago I was going to go to a workshop about bootstrap financing. I thought, "Oh, cool, I'll learn something there." I did learn something, but it was not what I thought. What I learned is that I was pretty good at this stuff already. They had all of these experts up there hem-hawing around. They didn't have it down to what I call a science. As they fumbled I was thinking, "No, first you do this and then you do that." I just wanted to jump up there and tell everybody how to 'bootstrap finance.' Being a business owner for a long time, I had actually developed seasoned skills by doing my own thing and networking with my own group. I didn't realize how much I had actually learned through my experience.

Bootstrap financing lets you maintain control over your company. Some people are willing to give it all away, but you can give away too much and still need more money. Without anything more to give away, suddenly you could find yourself with less and less control to the point you're just an employee on the project or your business halts. Just because you give away ownership, doesn't necessarily mean it's going to make it happen. When you hit roadblocks, you might find it's tempting to relinquish ownership and control of your company's direction. But analyze carefully if that is the best answer. Are you not qualified to carry the position? If not, what is the cost in removing from the helm the one with the dream/passion? If the project can not wait for your learning curve, arrange that you have good communication with whom you put at the helm, and find the proper position for yourself.

Protect your cash flow and use as much existing equipment and free resources as you can; whether borrowed equipment or public resources, i.e. the library or public agencies. Know when you have to make a small investment and re-feed your company with earnings you make. That's the main concept of bootstrap financing. By not borrowing money, you will work within your own resources and successes. Even if one feeds off the other, if you sell your car to buy some equipment, that's bootstrap financing. Walk around your house and find ways you can start up your project. Maybe it's a garage sale or setting monies aside from your current income sources. Basically, you need a commitment from yourself. How do you create initial commitment? Take something you believe in; then make small financial and time commitments. You'll find your passion and commitment to it will grow. If it's something you believe in, something that gives you passion, and you have more faith than fear (even if you need to remind yourself); it's going to come. Don't spend all your energy fretting that you can't start without a grant or a bank loan. If you aren't willing to sacrifice for your own ideas, don't bother asking someone else. Once you've put your money where your mouth is and sold what you can. The bank will probably expect you to mortgage your house or use your credit cards, before they accept the premise, "I've got a great idea. Give me the money." Please don't mortgage your house until you've got some business experience under your belt. Be careful with your credit; don't bet more than you are willing to lose but still balance it to show commitment to your project. (The larger the project – the more investors can look at the project's potential performance and your ability to perform; and less on your personal investment.)

Bootstrap financing, in the literal sense, is financing with all your own resources. I highly suggest that you do not leverage if you are new to business ownership and/or are financially inexperienced. Make your mistakes with your disposable income: through savings or liquidating assets. Even if you are experienced in business, leveraging requires careful thought.

Find the prime venue to your potential customer. The internet, direct marketing, vendor filled markets and trade shows are good resources for quick earning with limited commitment of capital outlay and long term lease agreements. You can bootstrap your project with preorders or commitment letters if your project isn't on the market yet or still in the development stage. Deposit any money collected in the development stage into a protected account for your customers. Ask your attorney for specific rules on the use and protection of such funds.

This is a great place to get creative and stand out from the crowd. Approach your customer with a sales concept that is from his vantage point. Create value for your customer. Maybe you can create marketing partnerships. In marketing this book, I called the marketing department of a paper company and asked if they'd be interested in a cooperative marketing campaign where they'd place a discount coupon for my book along with an online workshop on the boxes of their ream business paper which they sell in retail office supply stores. Motivating their customers to purchase their box of paper with this value added product. In return, I offered, if agreed, to pledge to choose a publishing/printing company that used their paper. So, I could use their paper for all my books!

That's just one example how the small company can work with the big company. The same is true in creative financing. My approach is team and partner with cooperative agreements. You are only limited by your imagination. This may be a great place to call me for individual consultation for advisory services but try to come up with some great ideas yourself.

Build creative partnerships and cooperative agreements where you are weakest. Whether you are raising capital, structuring distribution, building a sales team, purchasing material, or in research and development of your product or service; not having the money or resources may turn into an advantage in your execution to the market place, by becoming stronger and better than your competitors by sheer imagination.

Raising Capital and Creative Financing

_____

_____

_____

_____

_____

_____

_____

_____

_____

Oregon's Fortune Cookie

If you're a successful executive and you find yourself without a job, it can be unnerving and hard on the ego to do small projects to pull yourself up or to have to start from scratch with a totally new idea. A trick I've used is to make small business ventures, teaching moments for my kid. He can learn with me. Who knows? It may become a huge, successful project. If not, at least I taught my kid something. For example, my son and I got a Seattle City Pass and took several road trips north throughout the month I turned forty years old. I wanted to be close to him and create a positive memory for us to share. Weekend driving adventures, were great backdrops for creating a teaching moments about something dear to me, like how to think like an entrepreneur. It has given me such great joy, as I want him to know the skills to enjoy the free thinking experience also.

On our road trip, I played a "what if" game to illustrate a point: "If you ever found yourself homeless on the street, how might you be able to get back on your feet?" The first rule of the game is that you have to stay off of drugs and all of that. I started telling him about a product that I had developed after 9/11 while between jobs. Being Christmas time, I started thinking I had to buy Christmas presents for my extended family; and I didn't have extra money to do it. I never had been a real crafty person, but I was going to become a crafty person. As I walked around the house trying to figure out what I could make, I found some clam shells that I had collected. They had some sweet memories for me. As I studied them, I thought they reminded me of a fortune cookie. Playing with them, they seem to break as soon as I opened them up at the hinged part. So, I grabbed some silicone and glued it. It made the hinge flexible. I thought, "A fortune cookie needs a fortune in it." I got on the computer and typed some thought-filled inspirational messages and cut them into strips of paper ribbons. I folded the messages inside the clam shells and wrapped the outside of the shell with a paper ribbon that read, *Oregon's Fortune Cookie*. Since presentation is important, I placed them in a tissue filled Bon Marche box and mailed them off. My family called me quite enamored saying, "These are so wonderful."

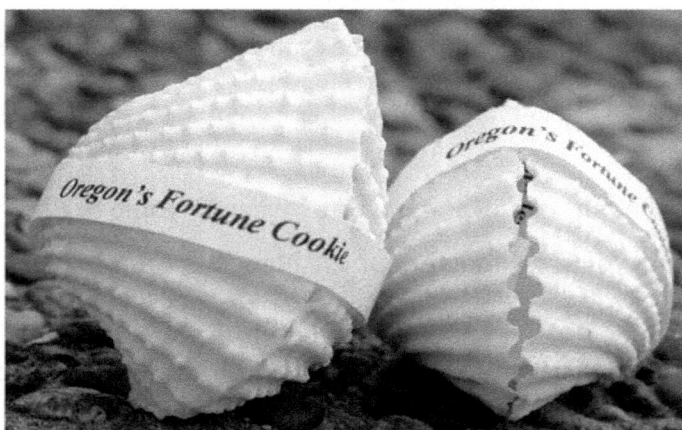

Copied with permission of Ehlmann Photography, Inc. copyright

94

Taking that idea, my son and I brainstormed. How could we take that idea and move from being a street peddler into full production? We thought after gathering shells we could start with handwritten messages or find a public library for our first production. Once enough sold we could upgrade the material quantity; by purchasing shells from craft wholesalers and add silicone at the hinge for quality. Although we left the first step of the street side vender to theory, we did make, market, and resell the product to retailers. Technically, the new entrepreneur could gross about $2500.00 (check your city – amounts vary) before a business license was required. Theoretically, the new entrepreneur could ask a fellow business owner to use or sublet a space (paid from a percentage of profits earned) so as not to break any city ordinances; or a bit more difficult, get a city permit to sell on public property.

Having never brought a product to market, we were curious to know how to take something from a basic idea and put it into production. Discovering what isn't in the text books, we worked on the packaging and marketing. We found an egg carton distribution company to pack the shells so as not to break them in shipping. We found a packing company for clear, individual bags to protect the message and ribbon label. We put the *Oregon's Fortune Cookie* in clear shiny bags and then topped it off with a folded thick paper label that read *Oregon's*

Fortune Cookie on the front and a legalese type safety label paraphrasing on the back, "Don't let anyone under five years old get a hold of it." We found that two 18-egg cartons fit perfectly into a US Post office priority mail box. We researched barcoding, then looked into merchant card services and website design for the future. Curiously for me, we didn't know anything about trademarks or copyrights, but we were able to research on the internet and trademark the name *Oregon's Fortune Cookie* for $25.00.

We developed an elevator pitch which described the product concisely in a short sales pitch. I remember actually giving an elevator pitch on an elevator ride once, back when promoting the Columbia River Project to an investment banker.

We found that wholesale buyers and store buyers rarely pass anything up, so as not to miss the next "pet rock" phenomena. But just because a buyer will buy it, does not necessarily mean the consumer will. They need to be sold on it. We decided to create a test market. We didn't want to market *Oregon Fortune Cookies* to a large store like Wal-Mart and have a mass production order, only to have a problem with the end user.

With a new product line, we had to set a value. Since this was a new product, we wanted to give it importance in quality of material, construction, marketing and packaging. The materials cost was still less than a dollar each, and overall took a couple of minutes to produce. Adding allowance for cost of future marketing, sales, rental space, shipping and billing time, we set the retail price at $5 each, which was comparable to shot glasses. We wanted to set the price high enough to allow liquidation of standing merchandising to still profit. We still needed to choose whether we'd market to unique boutique gift shops or to main stream, high volume gift stores, because unique gifts stores wouldn't buy if we sold to the main stream gift stores.

What we found was that when we got into the stores, the product moved slowly because they were not sitting you on the top front shelf, but rather on the bottom in the back corner. Plus, since it was not recognizable like a shot glass, people didn't know what it was; there was an education curve for the product. Once people figured out what it was, they sold pretty well. One main stream gift store questioned, if kids would play with them too much and whether the package would survive the school fieldtrip kids. It was nice to know that the buyers worried about the product would be too fun. The buyers for the Made in Oregon Stores liked our product but could not just buy one product. So they recommended that we take our time, develop a whole product line and requested that we represent.

While developing a full product line, we adjusted our market strategy for the *Oregon Fortune Cookie* to build product recognition and address the educational curve by selling to businesses that would not resell the product but be the end user. My thought was to market to high end resorts and spas to use as gifts for their guests. Instead of a mint on the pillow, they would have these little gifts or become part of gift baskets. If it worked in Oregon then we could imitate it in California, Washington and more. Many resorts liked the idea, but being only six months post 9/11, they wanted to wait until their industry got stronger. Unfortunately, the resort industry has been *in the tank* ever since, so the product has been put on hold. In the meantime, we learned the value of a test market; it allowed us to look at the timing, discover our errors, evaluate our market share, scale, and decide whether we're going to implement it again.

Since that time, I got a job in the architectural field again and moved on to other things. It was a fun learning experience with my kid and we made a few sales. We also had some nice perks, including traveling and basically sight seeing, while stopping at gift shops for sales. All legitimate tax-write offs (i.e. mileage, hotel stays, food) and it was fun. Someday we may continue with the idea.

Later, I asked my son, "Okay, it's your turn. What's your idea?"

He said, "To start a car magazine."

"What do you need first?"

"Car models!"

I laughed, "True, so true." I thought, "Perfect! He's developed an entrepreneurial mind!"

Today my son is eighteen and over the years I've enjoyed hearing about his career choices, whether cheer coach, marketing, pharmacist, pyrotechnic (movie special effects), professional bowler, apartment owner/developer or anything self-employed. He's very talented. He could choose many avenues. I'm sure you can make your dreams came true too, if you choose to love yourself. How do you do that? Remember to focus on your strengths.

Bootstrapping a service verses a product as first described usually requires less capital outlay. I still remember one day a friend of mine was working as a part-time retailer, living hand to mouth. The company wasn't giving her very many hours. I saw the fear in her eyes as she confided in me, "Cheri, I don't know if I'm going to make it." She was really frozen in fear, and I don't blame her. I found it really unnerving to see how much her self esteem and self worth was defined by this position that was making her feel worthless.

This job was not a good match. She was not living or working to her full potential. I told her, "If you do housekeeping to supplement your income, you can get $15 to $25 an hour. I mean look at it, you don't need a lot of education, you speak English; which is a bonus in the industry and you're a hard worker. Who knows, hook up a head set, record your thoughts as your working and write that book you've always dreamed of writing." She ran some ads and got herself into business as a housekeeper.

I still remember her calling me saying, "I've never been so happy in my life." The pride and control she felt from having her own company made her self esteem soar. When you realize that you are of infinite value and infinite worth, the sky's the limit.

Track My Progress | Test Market | Problems | Adjustment

_____

_____

_____

_____

Make Your Rain Dance

The simplest, funniest, craziest and most appropriate story to illustrate the right mindset to live your life and face the world as a leader is - from my kid. When he was about ten years old, I was going through a divorce. He noticed sadness in me. He came in the room determined to make me smile.

He said, "Mom, watch this. This is SO FUNNY!" As I watched my son, his face looked towards the ceiling with a fat tongue sticking out of his mouth, doing a sprinkler, spit flying, big motor sounding, raspberry with his mouth ""''b'l'a'a'blablablabalblablaballalalal'"'''''' ''' and turning himself around in circles. After about a minute of this, he proclaims, "It's a RAIN DANCE!" continuing in spit flying circles, elated with his discovery.

I said, "Clayton, that's NOT FUNNY. Cut it out."

"NO, NO Mom. It's FUNNY -watch!" and starts again ""''b'l'a'a'blablablabla'bla bla'blabla blablab l alal'''''''

"Clayton, it's not funny. Normally you're pretty funny but this is not funny. It's gross. CUT IT OUT!"

"No wait Mom, it's funny. ""''b'l'a'a'blablalal''' ""''b'l'a'a'blablablabla'b lab la'b labl ablablab lalal''''''''

We went back and forth but he wouldn't stop. Insisting, "Mom – just wait, really, this is so funny." And continued, """"b'l'aablablablablalab 'l'a'a'bl ablablab lablala b'l'aa'blablablablablalalb'l'a'a'blabl ablablab lalalb'l'a'a' blablablabl ablalalb'l'a'a'b ablalablablalab'l'a'a'babl all'""

After about 10 minutes of this I went from annoyed to mad. Yet a part of me admired the fact that even though he knew he could face corporal punishment for defiance, his agenda was determined - make mom happy. I started to consider his perspective. You know, after another five minutes, it was the funniest thing I'd ever seen. I was laughing so hard I fell off my chair and joined him in his dance.

So start your rain dance, have fun and follow YOUR dreams. Make a change, be a leader!

www.changeishardbooks.com

Published by Ehlmann Development, LLC

Want to purchase a book for someone else and let other know you care? Large order discounts available.

We have business participation fitting any budget from $32 to $5,000 and more. Advertising sponsors' cost of coverage equates to no more than 8 cents per book and can go as low as 3 cents per book for larger participation. We have programs placement for local/regional and national market distribution. Participant automatically qualifies into discount purchase plans for your employees, teams and/or customers.

For the reader: What now? Start leading your own life. Develop your plan. Outline key points in the book or call for a workshop and/or individual consultation. See our website for scheduling services.

Reference Material

"**Where is God When It Hurts**"
by Philip Yancey Zondervan Publishing House

"**The Little Engine That Could**"
by Watty Piper published by Platt & Munk

"**Organizing From the Inside Out**"
The Foolproof System for Organizing Your Home, Your Office and Your
Life By Julie Morgensern Simon and Schuster Audio

"**Rush Limbaugh's Address to the Nation**"
www.rushlimbaugh.com/home/daily/site_030209/content/
01125106.guest.html

Additional resources for **Michael Jackson**
www.michaeljackson.com/us/home /
www.latimes.com/entertainment/news/la-et-cause8-
2009jul08,0,369243.story

Additional resources for **Wal-Mart**
www.walmartstore.com / http://boingboing.net/2009/02/01/life-at-
walmart.html

Additional resources for **Sarah Palin**
www.sarahpac.com / www.facebook.com/sarahpal

Additional resources for **Ross Perot**
http://philanthropy.com/topdonors/gifts.php?view=topdonor&donor=PGDO
N4921&year=2008

Additional resources for **Changing the Tide**
www.oia.org Oregonians In Action
http://www.conservativetruth.org/article.php?id=118
http://www.infowars.com/a-message-to-the-environmental-movement-your-
movement-has-been-hijacked/

Additional resources for **Change is HARD/Self Reliance**
www.youmeworks.com/selfreliance.html
http://en.wikipedia.org/wiki/Individualism

Additional resources for **Ehlmann Photography, LLC**
www.ehlmann.com